The Humpback Whale

by Randy Frahm

Content Consultant:
Frederick Wenzel
Biology Department, Northeastern University
Member of Cetacean Society International

C A P S T O N E   P R E S S
M A N K A T O ,   M I N N E S O T A

C A P S T O N E   P R E S S
818 North Willow Street • Mankato, Minnesota 56001
http://www.capstone-press.com

Printed in the United States of America.

Library of Congress Cataloging-in-Publication Data
Frahm, Randy.
    The humpback whale/by Randy Frahm.
    p. cm.--(Wildlife of North America)
    Includes bibliographical references (p.45) and index.
    Summary: Details the characteristics, habitat, and life cycle of
the humpback whale.
    ISBN 1-56065-548-8
    1. Humpback whale--Juvenile literature. [1. Humpback whale.
2. Whales.]   I. Title.   II. Series.
QL737.C424F73   1998
599.5'25--DC21

                97-5968
                CIP
                AC

Photo credits
Bob Cranston, 6, 8, 11, 13, 14, 16, 21, 22, 24, 26, 29, 30,
   32-33, 34, 36, 39, 41, 42-43
Alberto Luca Reechi, cover

Table of Contents

Fast Facts about Humpback Whales

Scientific Name: *Megaptera novaeangliae*

Length: Males grow to about 45 feet (13 and one-half meters). Females grow to about 50 feet (15 meters) long.

Weight: An average humpback whale weighs between 25 and 45 tons (22 and one-half to 40 and one-half metric tons).

Range: Humpbacks can be found in all the world's oceans.

Habits: Humpback whales migrate during the year. Migrate means to leave one area at a certain time of the year to live somewhere else. Humpback whales migrate to different areas to find food, mate, and give birth to young.

Color: Humpback whales have gray or black bodies with white undersides.

Food: Humpbacks eat food found in the water. They eat small fish like anchovies and sardines. They also eat plankton and krill. Plankton is the mix of tiny animals and plants found in ocean water. Krill are very small shrimp.

Reproduction: Usually, humpbacks mate every year. Twelve months after mating, the female whale gives birth to a newborn whale that is called a calf.

Lifespan: Scientists believe humpbacks live from 30 to 80 years.

Chapter 1

The Humpback Whale

All whales are cetaceans. Cetacean means marine mammals including whales, dolphins, and porpoises. A mammal is a warm-blooded animal with a backbone. Warm-blooded means the body stays the same temperature no matter what the outside weather. Mammals give birth to live young. They have hair and breathe air.

Humpbacks are one kind of cetacean. They live in all of Earth's oceans. Humpbacks are different than other cetaceans. They perform special above-water behaviors. Other cetaceans are not as active as humpbacks.

Breaching is a special above-water behavior.

Humpbacks stick their tails out of the water to lob tail.

Special Behaviors

Breaching is one behavior humpbacks do above water. Breaching means jumping out of the water. Humpbacks usually land on their backs after breaching. Some humpbacks have breached as many as 100 times in a row.

Lob tailing is another humpback behavior. Humpbacks will stick their tails out of the water. They wave their tails back and forth.

Then they slap the surface of the water with their tails.

Another behavior humpbacks perform is flipper slapping. A flipper is the wide, flat limb of a sea creature. The front flippers of humpbacks are called pectoral flippers. Pectoral flippers help humpbacks keep their balance in the water. They also help humpbacks change direction when swimming.

Humpbacks swim near the water's surface when they want to slap their flippers. Then they turn on their side and wave one of their flippers in the air.

Humpback eyes are on the sides of their heads. They cannot always see things in front of them. Because of this, humpbacks spy hop when boats are close to them. To spy hop, humpbacks stick their heads out of the water. They use their tails to help them keep this position. Then they turn their heads to look at the boats.

Sometimes humpbacks perform several of these behaviors in a row. They also perform these behaviors in groups. A group of whales is called a pod.

Breathing

Humpback whales may look like fish, but they are really mammals. Because humpbacks are mammals, they must breathe air. Humpbacks dive underwater for three to 30 minutes. Then they come to the surface to breathe. They must sleep near the surface of the water, too. Otherwise, they would not be able to breathe.

Humpbacks breathe by using their blowholes. A blowhole is a hole on the top of a whale's head. A blowhole works like a human nose. It has two openings that let humpbacks suck in air. Humpbacks use their muscles to close and open their blowholes.

To breathe, humpbacks arch their bodies until their blowholes are out of the water. They blow old air out of their lungs. This shoots water and old air as high as 20 feet (6 meters) in the air. Then humpbacks fill their lungs with fresh air.

After taking three to seven breaths, humpbacks prepare to dive by bending their backs. Humpbacks bend their backs more than

Humpbacks blow old air out of their lungs.

other whales do. This humping or arching of their backs is one reason humpbacks received their name. The other reason is that humpbacks have a hump in front of their dorsal fin. The dorsal fin is the fin on a sea creature's back.

Appearance

Humpbacks have large, fish-like bodies. They are usually dark gray or black on the top and white on the bottom. Each humpback has a slightly different coloring.

Average adult humpbacks are from 39 to 50 feet (12 to 15 meters) long. Female humpbacks are usually larger than males. Females grow to about 50 feet (15 meters) long. Males grow to only about 45 feet (13 and one-half meters) long. Humpbacks have large heads that make up nearly one-third of their body length.

Humpbacks weigh between 25 and 45 tons (22 and one-half to 40 and one-half metric tons).

Humpbacks have a series of bumps called tubercles on their heads. One or two hairs grow from each tubercle. Scientists believe humpbacks use these hairs to sense motion in the water.

Flippers and Flukes

Humpbacks have the longest flippers of any kind of whale. Their flippers are one-third of their

Flippers help humpbacks balance while they swim.

bodies' length. The bones inside flippers look like the bones in human hands. Flippers help humpbacks keep their balance while they swim. Flippers also help humpbacks change direction in the water.

The trailing edge of humpbacks' fins are wavy. In the Pacific Ocean, the top side of humpbacks' flippers are gray or black. The

Humpbacks have 15 to 25 folds that swell when they eat.

undersides are white. In the Atlantic, both the tops and the undersides of the flippers are white.

Many people think humpbacks' flippers look like wings. In fact, their scientific name *Megaptera novaeangliae* means long-winged New Englander. A New Englander is someone who lives in the northeastern part of the United States. Many humpbacks are seen in New England waters.

Humpbacks also have tails that are called flukes. Flukes range in color from all black to all white. Sometimes they are part black and part white.

Most flukes are 10 to 12 feet (300 centimeters to 360 centimeters) wide. Flukes are V-shaped. Humpbacks move their flukes up and down. The up-and-down movements push humpbacks through the water.

Markings on the bottom side of flukes are like fingerprints on people. No two humpbacks have the same markings. Scientists photograph and collect the markings. That way, they can track humpbacks as the whales travel.

Folds and Baleen

Humpbacks' throats grow bigger when they eat. A group of 15 to 25 folds on their bodies help them do this. The folds run down the length of their bodies and stop near their stomachs. These folds stretch when humpbacks are feeding. Then humpbacks can swallow more food.

Barnacles attach themselves to the outside of humpbacks' folds. Barnacles only attach to slow-moving whales like humpbacks.

A humpback has 270 to 400 baleen in its mouth.

Barnacles are small shellfish. Shellfish are small sea creatures with shells. Humpbacks usually are not hurt by barnacles.

Baleen Whales and Toothed Whales

There are two kinds of whales. Toothed whales are whales that have teeth. Blowholes of toothed whales only have one opening for air. Toothed whales locate food by using echolocation. Whales send out clicks to begin the process of echolocation. The clicks travel through the water. They bounce off an object in the ocean. Then the clicking sounds travel back toward the whales. Whales can tell where an object is located by how long it takes the sounds to bounce back.

Baleen whales are the second kind of whales. Humpbacks are baleen whales. Baleen whales have two openings in their blowholes. They do not have teeth. Instead, they have baleen. Baleen is a long, thin bone that hangs on the inside of a whale's mouth. Rows of baleen line the inside of humpbacks' upper jaws and their mouths. The baleen looks like a mustache in the humpbacks' mouth.

Humpbacks may have from 270 to 400 baleen plates attached to their upper jaws. Each baleen is 33 to 40 inches (84 to 102 centimeters) long. Each baleen has bristles. These bristles help trap the small food that a humpback eats. Baleen can trap food that is less than an inch (about two centimeters) long.

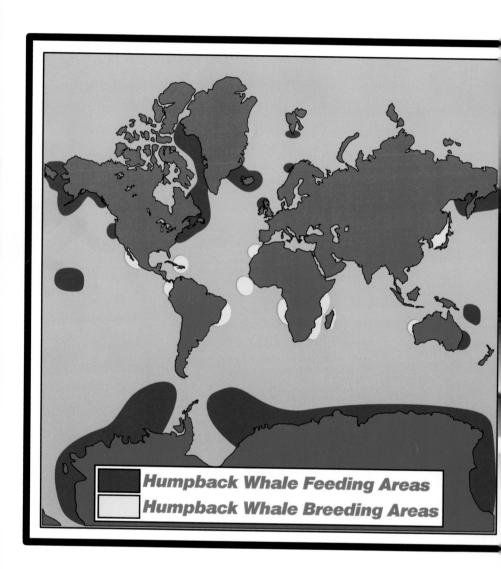

Humpback Whale Feeding Areas
Humpback Whale Breeding Areas

Chapter 2

Survival

Humpbacks do not stay in one area. Instead, they migrate. Migrate means to leave one area at a certain time of the year to live somewhere else. Humpbacks migrate to find food, mate, and give birth.

Migration

Humpbacks spend their summers in cold water. They migrate to areas that are full of food. In the North Atlantic, humpbacks migrate to Greenland, Iceland, Canada, and the waters around New England. In the North Pacific, the whales migrate to Alaska. Whales in the Southern Pacific migrate to Antartica and Australia.

Humpbacks spend their winters in warm water. They leave the cold areas and swim thousands of miles to warmer places. They mate and give birth in the warmer waters. Humpbacks in the North Atlantic migrate to Puerto Rico, the Dominican Republic, and other areas in the Carribean. Humpbacks in the North Pacific migrate to Hawaii, Mexico, and Japan.

Humpback migration takes 30 to 40 days. Humpbacks' bodies move slowly through the water. They swim only two to nine miles (three to 14 kilometers) per hour.

No one knows how humpbacks find their way from place to place. Scientists do know that humpbacks migrate through deep parts of the ocean.

Food

Humpbacks travel to the same cold-water feeding locations every summer. Sometimes there are more than 200 whales in a single feeding area. When they eat all the food in one area, they swim to another area. Their main foods are plankton

and krill. Plankton is the mix of tiny animals and plants that are found in ocean water. Krill are very small shrimp. Humpbacks also eat small fish like anchovies and sardines. Sometimes they eat fish like herring, pollock, and mackerel, too.

Humpbacks open their huge mouths when they feed. Their mouths are wide enough to hold a small car. But their throats are only as wide as a soccer ball. The baleen works like a filter. The krill and fish from the water are

trapped by the baleen. Humpbacks use their tongues to help them push this food down their small throats.

Catching Food

Humpbacks need to eat a lot. Their food is small, and they are huge animals. They eat nearly a ton (about one-half metric ton) of food every day. That much food is not always easy to find. So humpbacks catch food in several ways.

One way is to make a bubble net. To do this, humpbacks swim in circles beneath an area with fish. Then humpbacks release air from their blowholes. This makes bubbles. The bubbles can be very small or as large as basketballs. The size of the bubbles depends on the amount of air humpbacks release.

As humpbacks keep swimming, the bubbles form a kind of net around the fish. Sometimes the net can be as wide as 150 feet (45 meters). The bubble net scares the fish, and the fish form a tight school. A school is a group of fish. Then the humpbacks swim through the middle

Humpbacks make a bubble net to help them catch fish.

Blubber helps humpbacks float.

of the net with their mouths wide open. The scared fish become an easy meal.

At other times, humpbacks swim around fish. They slap the surface of the water with their flippers as they swim. This makes a ring of foam around the food. The ring scares and traps the food. After this, humpbacks dive underwater. Then they swim to the middle of the foam ring with their mouths open. Often humpbacks rise above the surface with their mouths wide open. Their baleen traps food as they rise.

Humpbacks often work together to catch food. A group of up to a dozen humpbacks locates an area that has food. The whales then work together to move the food into one spot. Finally, the whales rush into the food-filled area with their mouths open.

Blubber

Humpbacks eat often during the summer. They eat to make blubber. Blubber is fat. Humpbacks use blubber during migration when they cannot find their regular food. Their bodies then use blubber for energy.

Blubber helps humpbacks in other ways, too. It keeps them warm. It shields them against the cold water. Blubber also helps humpbacks float. This is because blubber is lighter than water.

Chapter 3

The Humpback Whale's Life

Humpbacks make different noises to communicate with each other. They grunt, click, or make a chirp-like sound. Humpbacks usually make these sounds during migration and in their summer feeding areas.

Humpbacks also use noises in another way. They put different sounds together to make songs. Humpback songs can travel up to six miles (10 kilometers) underwater. Some scientists believe that only males sing.

When male humpbacks begin to sing, they stop in the water. They put their heads lower

Humpbacks make noises to communicate with each other.

than their tails and stretch out their flippers.
This helps them stay in one place in the water.

Humpback Songs

Most scientists believe that males sing to attract
females. This is because humpbacks usually sing
during mating season.

Humpbacks can sing for many hours. Each
song lasts seven to 15 minutes. Humpbacks
sing a series of sounds in the same order. They
string together many series of sounds to form
a song.

All the humpbacks that live in the same area
of the ocean sing the same song. The song in
each area changes every year.

Scientists record and study humpback songs.
They can identify humpback migration patterns
by humpbacks' songs. They can also identify
the year the song was sung. But scientists do
not know why or how the song changes every
year. They do not know how all humpbacks in
an area know the song.

Mating

Humpbacks migrate to their mating areas every winter. These mating areas are called breeding grounds. Humpbacks that feed near Alaska in the summer migrate to the same winter breeding grounds. These are near Mexico, Hawaii, or Japan. Humpbacks that feed off New England, Canada, Iceland, and Greenland migrate to the Carribean.

Calves surface to breathe every two to five minutes.

Humpbacks do not mate for life. The female humpback chooses a male for mating. The chosen male is called the primary escort. He travels with the female whale. Sometimes this can become difficult. Other males want to mate with the female, too. Primary escort males must often fight with other males.

Males make their throats swell to appear larger. They do this to scare other males. Fighting males ram their heads into each other's bodies. They hit each other with their tails. Barnacles on the tails sometimes cut fighting humpbacks. Because of this, male humpbacks have more scars than females.

Calves

Females usually give birth every other year. However, some female humpbacks give birth every year.

Twelve months after mating, females will migrate to warm water. There they give birth. Young humpbacks are called calves.

Calves are born underwater. Their mothers probably help them to the surface for their first breaths. After that, calves must swim to the surface to breathe every two to five minutes.

Newborn calves are 12 to 16 feet (four to five meters) long. They weigh from one to two tons (about one to two metric tons). Calves nurse on their mothers' thick milk. The milk is 50 percent fat. Human females' milk is usually no more than 20 percent fat.

Young calves may gain more than 50 pounds (22 kilograms) a day. After five months, calves

Sometimes male humpbacks act as an escort.

begin eating the adult humpback diet of fish, krill, and plankton.

Sometimes a male humpback will travel with a mother and a calf. The male usually

protects the other whales. The humpback male
may not be the calf's father, but he helps
protect the calf. Some scientists think the male
hopes to mate with the female.

Chapter 4

Past and Future

Whales have existed for thousands of years.
Many native peoples of North America tell
stories about whales. The Inuit (IN-oo-it) people
are natives of northern Canada and the Arctic.
They were once known as Eskimos. Whales were
an important source of food for the Inuit. They
tell this story to explain how whales were created.

Once there was a girl named Sedna. She was
tricked into marrying a bird that had disguised
itself as a handsome man. She was very
unhappy. One day, her father came to visit.
Sedna decided to leave with her father. Her
bird husband would not let her leave. So Sedna
killed the bird.

Whales have existed for thousands of years.

Killer whales sometimes attack young humpbacks.

She and her father got on a boat and left for home. Other birds found out about the murder. They caused a terrible storm. Sedna's father threw her overboard so the storm would stop. Sedna tried to hold on to the boat, but her father cut off each of her fingers. Each finger turned into an animal that lived in the sea. Her fingers turned into a whale, a seal, a dolphin, a fish, and a manatee.

Sedna became the goddess of the sea. The whale was her most powerful subject.

Humpback Enemies

Scientists believe that humpbacks live for 30 to 80 years. They have only a few natural enemies.

Killer whales sometimes attack young humpbacks. Scientists often see bite marks from killer whales on the tails of humpbacks. Even so, people have been humpbacks' worst enemies.

Whaling

Humans once hunted whales for many reasons. The hunting of whales is called whaling. People who hunt whales are called whalers.

People eat whale meat. In the past, they also used whale oil in margarine and lamps. People ground whale bones into fertilizer. Fertilizer is something put on land to make crops grow better. People used baleen to make umbrellas, buggy whips, and hoop skirts.

The first whalers tried to kill whales with harpoons. Harpoons are long spears with ropes attached to them. Whalers tried to stick their harpoons into whales.

For many years, whaling was not a threat to whale populations. But as time went on, whaling ships became larger and faster. They were able to catch more whales.

International Whaling Commission

People were concerned because so many whales were being killed. The International Whaling Commission formed in 1946. Its job was to help control whaling and protect whales.

Whaling severely reduced humpback populations. There were about 22,000 Antarctic humpbacks in 1930. By 1965, that population was down to 3,000. Humpbacks were in danger of becoming extinct. Extinct means no longer living or existing.

The International Whaling Commission wanted to protect humpbacks. In 1966, it helped pass a law. The law made it illegal to hunt humpbacks in all the oceans of the world.

It is hard to count humpbacks because oceans are so huge, and the whales move often.

Future

Today, humpbacks are still considered an endangered species. An endangered species is one in danger of becoming extinct.

It is difficult to know how many humpbacks are alive today. It is hard to count humpbacks because the oceans are so huge and humpbacks move often. Some scientists say there are between 8,000 and 10,000 humpbacks left.

Others believe that there are at least 35,000 humpbacks.

Scientists know that humpback populations are becoming larger. This is because it is illegal for whalers to hunt humpbacks.

Whale Watching

Today, humpbacks are popular for whale watchers. Millions of people around the world are whale watchers. They buy tickets to sail on boats that get close to whales. In one year, more than 3.5 million North Americans spent $46 million on whale watching.

There are many places to watch whales. During the summer, people in Maine, Massachusetts, and New Hampshire have good locations for watching humpbacks. Canadians in Newfoundland, Quebec, and Nova Scotia have many opportunities to watch whales, too. In winter, people who live in Hawaii, Puerto Rico, and Mexico can enjoy whale watching.

Future

The success of whale-watching businesses shows that protecting endangered animals can help provide jobs. Whale watching also helps people learn more about humpbacks.

Scientists still have much to discover about humpback whales. They have questions about humpback mating, migration, and songs. They also want to study the reasons why humpbacks breach and lob tail.

It is important to keep oceans clean. Polluted water can hurt humpbacks and their food. Keeping water clean will protect whales in all the world's oceans. Then humpbacks can stay healthy. Scientists will be able to learn more about humpbacks.

Eye

Folds

Flipper

Fluke

Words to Know

baleen (BAY-leen)—a long, thin piece of bone attached to the mouths of some whales
barnacle (BAR-nuh-kuhl)—a small sea creature with a shell
blubber (BLUH-bur)—fat used by whales for energy, floating, and keeping warm
breaching (BREECH-ing)—when a whale leaps out of the water
calf (KAF)—a young whale
flipper (FLIP-ur)—the wide, flat limb of a sea creature
fluke (FLOOK)—a whale's tail
harpoon (har-POON)—a long spear with an attached rope
krill (KRIL)—a very small shrimp
lob tailing (LOB TAYL-ing)—when whales stick their tails out of the water and slap them
migrate (MYE-grate)—to leave one area at a certain time of the year to live somewhere else

To Learn More

Bright, Michael. *Humpback Whale*. New York: Gloucester Press, 1990.

Gohier, Francois. *Humpback Whales: Traveling on the Wings of Song*. Parsippany, N.J.: Silver Burdett Press, 1995.

Palmer, Sarah. *Humpback Whales*. Vero Beach, Fla.: Rourke Enterprises, 1988.

Patent, Dorothy Hinshaw. *Humpback Whales*. New York: Holiday House, 1989.

Prevost, John. *Humpback Whales*. Edina, Minn.: Abdo and Daughters, 1995.

Wexo, John Bonnett. *Whales*. Mankato, Minn.: Creative Education, 1990.

Useful Addresses

American Cetacean Society
P.O. Box 2639
San Pedro, CA 90731

Cetacean Society International
P.O. Box 953
Georgetown, CT 06829

Institute of Ocean Sciences
9860 West Saanich Road
P.O. Box 6000
Sidney, British Columbia V8L 4B2
Canada

National Marine Fisheries Services
Office of Public Affairs
Department of Commerce
Washington, DC 20235

Internet Sites

Cetacean Page Just for Children
http://www.premier1.net/~iamdavid/children.
  html

Cetacean Society International
http://elfnetla.elfi.com/csihome.html

OceanLink—Marine Science
http://oceanlink.island.net/index.html

Save the Whales
http://www.tmarts.com/savethewhales

The Virtual Whale Project
http://fas.sfu.ca/cs/research/projects/Whales/

WhaleNet
http://whale.wheelock.edu/

Index